CHURCH SECURITY

PROVIDING A SAFE WORSHIP ENVIRONMENT

KEVIN ROBERTSON

DIRECTOR OF SECURITY FOR SADDLEBACK CHURCH

Church Security
Providing a Safe Worship Environment

pastors.com

Requests for information should be addressed to:

Pastors.com
30021 Comercio
Rancho Santa Margarita, CA 92688

ISBN: 978-1-4228-0316-5

Printed in the United States of America.

TABLE OF CONTENTS

Introduction 3

Chapter 1
Is There Really a Need? 5

Chapter 2
Building the Foundation as a Ministry 11

Chapter 3
Where to Start 23

Chapter 4
Equipping a Team.. 31

Chapter 5
Training a Team... 43

Chapter 6
It's All About the Kids.. 53

Chapter 7
Handling Disruptions 59

Chapter 8
Soft Target/Hard Target 63

Chapter 9
Partnering With Local Resources 67

Chapter 10
Security Cameras.. 71

Acknowledgements 75

Introduction

It is my hope, my desire, and my prayer that as you read this book, you will be able to glean some things out of it to help your church's security ministry. In life there are Shepherds—those God created to take care of his people, the pastors and ministers who help people come to know God and help them grow closer to God in their daily walk. Then there are the Sheep, who love God with all their heart and step up to the plate every day to express their love for him and for others. And lastly there are Sheepdogs. Though they're smaller in number, God has SHAPE'd (a term my pastor, Rick Warren, came up with: Spiritual Gifts, Heart, Abilities, Personality, and Experiences) them for this role. They are the ones who stop those that would pursue harmful thoughts and deeds and declare, "Not here, not at my church, not to those I've been entrusted to care for." To me they are heroes, such incredible servants, and they are the reason I wrote this book.

Over the years I have been so blessed to be able to serve at Saddleback Church, and through this I have had the opportunity to meet so many peers all across the country. So many church security team leaders, whether paid or volunteers (the real heroes), have become close friends of mine. I have learned from them, been encouraged by them, and valued their friendship and prayer support.

I have had an amazing secular career journey, but it doesn't even come close to what I am able to do today as a part of the team at Saddleback Church. It is a privilege and a blessing that I don't take lightly—or for granted. It is my passion to not only provide as safe and as disturbance-free worship environment as possible for our campuses, but also to tell my peers about any learnings we've had, the things we tried that didn't work, and the ideas that did work. As my pastor says, "We're all on the same team; we're not in competition with each other. We've got to help each other out." So blessed to be a blessing.

Saddleback Church Security Ministry Purpose Statement

To provide a safe and secure environment for the children and adult members of Saddleback Church and the guests and visitors to ensure that their Saddleback experience is one that can focus on their spiritual growth and worship time. To be as "wise as serpents and as gentle as doves."

To ensure as best as we can as disturbance-free of a worship experience as possible for those who come onto any of our campuses. If and when a disturbance does arise, our goal is to remove that disturbance in a Christ-like way and in a manner that is the very least attention-attracting to the situation as possible so that those attending the event go quickly back to focusing on why they are there.

1

Is There Really a Need?

Before I go any further I want to make one thing clear, something I share with leaders at every church I talk with. This book is filled with things that work for us at Saddleback Church—and, of course, also the things we tried that didn't work. It is my hope and my prayer that you can glean some ideas for your security team. Use some of these ideas, modify whatever you need to fit your particular church, and create your own security team—a team that's specifically designed for what works in your church. A style of security team that works for Saddleback Church, or a church in Paris, Tennessee, or a church in Newark, New Jersey, will vary just as much as people's accents do. What is constant is the need to provide as safe and as disruptive-free environment as possible for people to gather and worship God.

In speaking to pastors at churches around the country and at church conferences, I can't tell you how many times I've heard "Our church is in a nice part of town; we don't worry about crime" or "We're in a small, rural area; that's a big-city church problem." But the fact that we're talking or they've come to a conference is a good sign—that's a start. A few years ago, I met with a group of pastors who were considering church security;

they flew me out to talk with them about it. About five minutes into our conversation, I could tell that a couple of them really weren't on board with the need for security at their churches.

One pastor said, "Well, our church is not really in what you would call a high-crime area; I'm not sure if we really have a need." I thought, *Okay that's a low-hanging curveball; I can't let that one go by without swinging at it.* So I responded, "That's great! I'm glad you're in a low-crime area. Tell me, as the senior pastor, do you ever counsel couples at your church?" He replied, "Yes, off and on." "Okay," I responded, "in your counseling experience with couples, have you ever had a time when any physical abuse was involved?"

It turns out that just a few months earlier, they had a situation with a couple who were members of that church. The husband had a drinking problem and, apparently, quite a temper, too. A few weeks into counseling with this couple, the wife called the church because the husband had been drinking, got angry with her and the kids, backhanded her, knocked her down, and she ended up with a black eye.

I asked, "So what'd you do?"

He said, "Well, we checked her and the kids into a hotel near the church. We tried to talk with him, but he was still drunk. We figured we'd let him sleep it off and we'd go over and talk with him after church, since this happened on a Saturday night. Our plan was to get him some help, get them some additional counseling, and hopefully restore their marriage.

"Unfortunately, we later found out he started drinking again in the morning. He called his wife's cell phone, and she said the church put her and the kids up in a hotel—they'd be fine and she wasn't going to talk to him until he was sober. Well, he showed up right in the middle of our service—drunk and shouting all kinds of obscenities and saying we told his wife to divorce him."

Needless to say, this pastor's story grabbed everyone's attention.

This guy was pretty upset, and the pastor said he'd never seen such anger. After yelling some more obscenities, the man finally left. Afterward, the pastor and some other leaders were talking about it and someone said, "I'm sure glad he didn't bring one of his guns with him."

That led me to my next question for the pastor: "So, what would you guys have done if he'd brought a firearm? What was your plan?" The pastor paused for a moment, slowly shook his head, and said, "You know what, until this moment, I have to say that never occurred to us. I now know we would have had no idea what to do, and thank God that didn't happen. If he had brought a gun, I'm afraid a lot of people might have been hurt—or worse."

This was an "aha" God moment. Now these pastors were ready to do what they could to protect the people God had entrusted to their care—not only to shepherd them as they grew in spiritual maturity, but keep them as safe as they possibly could from wolves that would seek to harm them or, at the very minimum, disrupt their time to worship God.

When I travel around the country speaking to churches about church security, very rarely do I bring up church crime statistics. Why? Unless we're mentally ready to buy in to the concept of church security, we can always rationalize away the statistics. Here's an example from another area of life: *I don't need to buy flood insurance for our home. It's been over 100 years since we had a flood here. Floods happen mostly in other parts of the state.* We've all had thoughts and rationalizations like that at one time or another.

When churches ask me about church security, I try to approach it from a biblical standpoint. I see this as one more example of God knowing what he was doing when he took a former cop, turned him into a pastor, and then the head of security at a church. For me, this is the easiest and best part to talk about. Sure, there are the technical and the tactical components, which are fun and important parts. But as a pastor I look at church security as stewardship. As pastors we love God and love people. God has called us to serve in the role of shepherds, where we can passionately love and care about people.

Sometimes we get tunnel vision and only focus on the spiritual growth and maturity of those we're shepherding. And while that's an extremely important and foundational piece, we can't lose sight of the fact there are other parts of the puzzle that complement, support, or provide the environment for spiritual growth to happen.

I could give you all kinds of church crime stats and examples. But as I tell my team, we can change people's heads, but that change won't last. They'll likely end up back with their old behavior. However, if we can change their hearts, then they've got it for life.

Whether you already have a church security ministry at your church and are looking to improve, or you are starting from scratch, it is my hope and my prayer that you will come to see church security the same way God placed it on my heart: as a ministry. It's not something we do because we feel we have to. We do it because we so love people we want to provide them with as safe and undisruptive a place as we possibly can so they can grow closer to God. I hope that you come to see that having a security ministry at your church doesn't mean you're paranoid or extremist.

You and I are just preparing for the worst while praying for the best. And we're not sticking our heads in the sand. It's a biblical balance. We're being as wise as serpents and as gentle as doves at the same time. And this is so doable; I watch our security team at Saddleback do this every day.

2

Building the Foundation as a Ministry

I think one of the main stumbling blocks for implementing security at a church is the inner struggle we face as Christians. We want to be open and welcoming to all. We want to turn the other cheek. We are committed to opening our church doors to everyone. But if we're totally honest, if we saw that same person on the street while driving our car late at night, we might find ourselves subconsciously reaching to lock the door.

Too often we view security at our churches from one extreme or the other. Either we have a lockdown mentality—with draw bridges, moats, alligators, and armed bar-bouncer types—or we go to the other extreme and stick our heads in the sand. I believe we can find a biblical balance. Somewhere in the middle, we can be open and inviting while keeping people as safe as possible and providing as much of a disruption-free worship experience as we possibly can.

As the head of security at Saddleback Church, I've learned that our security ministry is a constantly growing, learning, and evolving thing. Like many churches across the country, we didn't start a security team because of a huge situation. It was something that someone proposed and we've gone with it. We've made mistakes, found things that worked, and found many others that didn't work. Because many of us on the team have a law enforcement background, we rely on those experiences—not to create a police force, but to use our trainings and experiences to create a security team.

One day I was preparing to speak on church security to a group of pastors at a conference at the Long Beach Convention Center. I was going over my notes, sorting out the topics to cover. I'd done these conferences many times and always enjoyed doing them. All of sudden I realized that I was going down the "technical" road. I'd gotten so focused on the nuts and bolts that I'd lost sight of the fact that we were talking about *church security*.

I stopped typing and started talking to God. I remember saying, "God, I'm trying to do this the way I think it should be done. I'm trying to put together a church security team, a team that can protect and serve. But what I really want is to do this your way, to build a team where we can serve you. Please show me the way." God reminded me that not only had he given me my law enforcement experiences that would help, he had also created me to be a pastor—and the pastor in me saw this as a ministry. This was my "aha" moment. I realized that this needed to be the foundation; it needed to be a ministry. It might seem like just a word, a security *ministry*, but it changes the focus completely. So security at Saddleback Church is all about ministry.

When we're recruiting team members, we tell them we are flexible in some areas, but in two specific areas we're not. First, everyone we interact with will be treated in a Christ-like way—it's all about grace. I've seen our team members do this time and time again: be as wise as serpents and as gentle as doves at the same time. Second, they need to be comfortable with praying with someone.

That's it—the two areas where there's no flexibility. As a matter of fact, we meet one-on-one with each potential new team member—paid or volunteer—and explain that we have one important question. Many people on our team have told us afterward that they thought this would be some form of tactical question. But here's the question we ask them: "Are you willing to pray with someone?" For some, this is an easy yes; for others, it's a little out of their comfort zone, but they're willing. We can work with a heart like that.

Let me give you two examples where this foundation came into play. My first example is a guy named Randy, who was paranoid, schizophrenic, off his medication by choice, alcoholic, and homeless. Randy was offered help by many different ministries at Saddleback, including Celebrate Recovery, Pastoral Care, and our Minister of the Day.

However, he had no interest in getting better or taking their recommendations. Eventually he was told that unless he got back on his medication and off the alcohol, he was no longer allowed on the church property. During that period of time, our night security team members found him on campus at least a half-dozen times.

His intent was to find an unlocked door and spend the night. Each time one of our security team members would find him we'd escort him off the campus. But it was always done in a Christ-like manner. So they were being as wise as serpents and as gentle as doves. One time we found him, along with two other homeless guys, in an unlocked classroom; they had a jug of wine, a carton of cigarettes, and a small barbecue. They planned to spend the night and put leaves and twigs in the barbecue and light them to make things "cozy." Needless to say, we let them know they couldn't do this.

About six months later on a Sunday morning, I saw Randy on campus, but this time he looked different. His long hair was clean and combed, and his clothes were clean and pressed. He walked up to me, stuck his hand out to shake mine, and said, "I need to apologize to you and your team for all the grief I caused you this past year. I've gotten back on my medication, got a place to live and a job, and I haven't had a drink in four months."

Imagine if Randy had experienced a heavy-handed security team at Saddleback Church during his EGR time (a phrase Pastor Rick Warren uses when a person is "Extra Grace Required"): one that grabbed him by the collar, threw him off campus, and called the police. Once he got his life turned around, his thought might have been, "Forget those Christians—been there, done that." A couple of years have gone by, and Randy's still doing well and remains involved at Saddleback Church. This just solidified in our mind that viewing security as a ministry is the right approach. Does this mean that every person is going to turn around? Not necessarily. But we definitely want to do all we can to treat them in a Christ-like way.

My second example also took place a few years ago. One of our security team members came across a woman in her late 20s on the main patio. It was about 11 p.m.; she was upset and crying. In talking with her, our team member learned that she and her fiancé had had an argument and she just needed a quiet place to pray, so she had come to that spot. Our security team member did four things, which exemplify our security ministry.

- First, he gave her the phone number for the church office and encouraged her to call the Pastoral Care team in the morning. He told her we had premarital counseling, and whether she and her fiancé were members or not, someone would be more than happy to talk with them.

- Second, he suggested that she move to an area on the other side of the patio (for her safety) where she'd be sitting under a light.
- Third, he did what is so typical for our security team members: He prayed with her.
- Fourth, after talking with this woman, he went back to the security vehicle and parked far enough away that she could have some privacy, but close enough that he could still see her. She stayed for about a half-hour; he waited until she'd gotten to her car and was heading off, and then his job was done.

When he relayed this story to me the following day, I realized that this was textbook—this was perfect. As a security team member, he saw someone on the campus late at night and checked it out to make sure the campus was safe. And then, more importantly, as a minister he gave her guidance, prayed with her, and then ensured she was safe while she had some quiet time with God.

This is why it's a ministry.

People from other churches have asked me about our thoughts on using an outside security guard company. At one point we tried this, and it provided some advantages. However, for our particular needs, some things just didn't work (I'll explain more in a moment). We contracted with a couple of different security guard companies over the course of a year to cover our graveyard shifts when we were shorthanded when a team member was sick or on vacation.

Before I go any further, please understand that what I'm about to say is not meant to demean or disrespect security guards. They're great at what they do. But for us, it didn't work and doesn't work. Let me explain why. First, think about the scenario with the upset woman on our campus late at night. A security guard running across the same situation might approach the woman and, in a very nice way, tell her that the campus is closed and she'd have to leave. If she wanted to talk with someone, she'd have to come back tomorrow when the church was open.

Now technically, this would all be correct. Our campus does close at 10 p.m. or 11 p.m., depending on the night of the week. So he would be following instructions. But in a church setting, things need to be handled with grace.

Or in the other scenario, a security guard might act differently to protect the property of a client. If Randy showed up with the intent of "camping overnight," the security guard probably would have called the police. Again, nothing against them—they're doing their job by being security "guards."

Let's consider one last possibility. Let's say you contract with a security guard company. Perhaps they send out a guard who is not a Christian. He interacts with a first-time visitor or a member of your church and, for whatever reason, is a bit heavy-handed verbally.

The perception will be that security at your church was rude. It doesn't matter if people know or don't know that it's an outside service. The interaction happened on your property so he's yours—you own it. As the old saying goes, perception is reality.

That's why for us, a security guard won't work out. Once again, this is what works and doesn't work for us. You need to pray about it, talk about it, and figure out what works best for you and your church.

In order to serve on our security team at Saddleback, either paid or as a volunteer, a person must be a member of Saddleback. I have a couple of Christian friends who are both retired from law enforcement. Early on we kicked around the idea of using them on our security team as independent contractors. But they're members of another church, and we realized they'd really just be doing a job. For our team members, it's a completely different perspective. This is their church family; this is their church home that they're serving to protect.

We're always looking for ways to improve, and God is constantly showing us these areas. Sometimes what might seem like a small idea or observation can be another foundational piece. On a typical Sunday morning, we will post six security team members inside our worship center (in addition to the members of our Law Enforcement Ministry, which I'll talk about in a later chapter). We'll have one on each side, two in plain clothes seated in the ends of the front row, and two in the rear of the worship center (one on each side).

One weekend as I sat there in the service with my wife, I looked at our team members, trying to view them from the perspective of a first-time guest or a member. The team members on each side of the worship center are seated on a stool when the church is seated, and when the attendees stand to sing, the security team members stand, too, so they can maintain their view of the worship center. They wear shirts with "Saddleback Church Security" embroidered on the front, but it's not too big—it's there, but it doesn't "scream" security. This doesn't seem heavy-handed, but it does help me feel like I'm in a secure environment.

As we all started to sing, it hit me: Our security guys are doing their job, they're keeping an eye on what's going on, but something seemed missing. In that moment, God reminded me that it's a ministry—not just for how our security team is perceived, but also how team members perceive their role. After the service I found our security team leader, Gina Minnis, and told her that I'd like our team members that serve inside the worship center—or any of our other venues—to sing when the congregation is singing.

This would serve two purposes. First, if you're a first-time guest, seeing a security team member might make you wonder if there had recently been a problem that warranted a security presence. But as the music starts and the people begin singing, and you see the security team member singing also, it removes some of the visual intimidation. These guys are here just like the ushers and the greeters—they're serving. The second purpose benefits our team, especially for those with a law enforcement background: It's tough for a heart to be hardened as you look for "bad guys" while you're singing praise songs.

Sure, I got a couple of groans from our "non-singing" team members, but we tell them in a crowd of 3,000, no one's going to hear if they're off-key. What they will see is you participating in the service right alongside them. A caveat to this: When our guys are serving, they don't take notes (fill-ins on the message handout) along with the rest of the congregation. They need to be focused on the task at hand, and taking notes during the message can be a distraction.

Let me talk for a moment about how you might handle minor distractions during your service. We have several video-based regional campuses. One Sunday morning, during the message, one of the attendees responded back to comments Pastor Rick made in his message. It seemed as if the guy believed Pastor Rick was speaking to him directly—even though our pastor was on video, not there in person. It was just a word or two and nothing rude or obnoxious. After the service I looked for him on the patio outside, spoke with him, and got to know him. He hadn't been coming to our church for very long. It was obvious he loved God and simply struggled with an issue where he would shout out things. We talked about how we loved having him worship with us, how we wanted him to be a part of our Saddleback Church family, and also explained how some people might find his comments distracting while they're listening to the pastor's message.

He said he fully understood; we hugged, and I prayed with him and told him I'd hope to see him the following weekend. He did return the following weekend and subsequent weekends, and this issue only came up one more time, about a month later. He and I spoke again; he apologized, and it hasn't happened since. To this day he attends services each weekend and always gives me a hug when we see each other.

I think the learnings here are multiple. First, sometimes our kneejerk response is to overreact. We could have approached this man during the service and asked him to be quiet or asked him to leave, but that would've drawn more attention to the situation and would've distracted from the service even more. Second, we sometimes can find our best solutions by taking some time after the fact, building a "bridge" and a relationship with the person, and finding out where they're coming from. Three, you have to make a judgment call based on each particular situation. It's wise to have a general plan, but our security team members and our ushers must discern how to handle each situation—and no two situations will be alike. We have written guidelines that spell out how to handle these situations, but they are just that: guidelines.

We choose to focus more on doing scenario training (I'll talk more about training in a bit).

We should never get so "black and white" in how we handle EGR ("Extra Grace Required") people that we forget that this is a ministry. Our goal as a security team is never to kick people off our campus. If someone is being disruptive or displaying inappropriate behavior, we'll ask them to stop that behavior or they'll need to leave and come back another day. We ultimately want them back. As my pastor says, "The church is not a place for saints to hang out; it's a hospital for sinners." We want people to leave their inappropriate behavior "at the door" and worship God alongside us.

I tell our teams and other churches: Let your ushers be the first line of defense, not security. Here's a situation that explains why. I was working with a church in the Midwest, helping them to refine their security ministry, which was fairly new. I'd flown out to visit them for their weekend services and then to meet with them and brainstorm the following week. As people were singing during one of their services, everyone was standing, a few with arms stretched high toward the heavens. I noticed a guy near the front of the auditorium had stepped up onto his chair—singing with the rest of us, but just with a bit more "altitude." Within a few seconds, two of the church's security team members approached him, one of them spoke with him, and he stepped down from the seat and continued to sing, as the security team members went back to where they were posted.

At our meeting the following Monday morning, I asked the leaders about this incident. Had they experienced problems with him being disruptive in the past? Had they had instances in the past where other people had been disruptive? I was trying to understand where they were coming from and their reasoning for the way it was handled. No, this was the first time for that person, and they hadn't experienced any disruptive problems in the past. They said they were just trying to be proactive.

I told them I believed being proactive was a great thing. I simply wanted to discuss some alternative ways they might handle those types of situations in the future. First of all, for someone that's not trying to disrupt the service maliciously but is maybe just a little "distracting" for those around them, ushers can be the first line of defense, not security. In most cases, the person would be more receptive to a gentle "guiding" from an usher than a confrontation with security.

Secondly, let's view it from a first-time guest's perspective. If a new family had been in that service, the guy standing on his seat might have been a little odd and a little distracting. But when security team members step in, they might think, "So the guy was a little passionate; it wasn't like he just robbed a convenience store. Was security really needed?" On the other hand, an ushers-first approach might have produced a thought of, "Wow, that guy was passionate about his singing, but it was nice of that usher to talk to him; it was a little distracting having him standing on his chair in front of us."

This is just one more of the ways at Saddleback where we purposely strive to build and use our security team as a ministry and look for any areas where it might possibly be misinterpreted as heavy-handed.

3

Where to Start

This is probably the most frequently asked question I get: "Where do I start?" Right up there with it is the statement "We have no budget for this." Understandably, on face value this can seem like an overwhelming task. However, in reality it's just the opposite. As to the cost factor, I've heard this so many times from so many churches, and my answer is always the same: It doesn't take any money to start up a security ministry.

I've traveled around the country to help churches set up security ministries. One of the things I enjoy most is meeting with a church and finding out their biggest concern is the start-up cost—and by the end of the day we've laid out a start-up security ministry with zero money out of pocket. Of course, as they progress there'll be things they want to budget for, but to start up, you just need people willing to serve.

Begin by determining the areas you need to secure. My encouragement for you would be to consider starting with these three areas: your children's area, your main worship center, and the area you process your offering. These are the areas where you're most likely to face a problem.

Plan a meeting with your staff or your lay leaders to start your brainstorming. Do you have any members of your church that are either current or former law enforcement? If so, put them on your list of potential security team members. If not, that's okay; you can still move forward.

One quick suggestion as you start building your team, talking among your members, advertising in the bulletin, and spreading the word: Hold off on appointing a leader for a while. I helped a church on the East Coast with a fairly new security ministry. Once they decided to start, they found the first person that was interested and made them the leader. It worked out okay for a short period of time, but as they acquired more team members, they realized the team leader was not wired for that role.

As a side note, I'd encourage you to check out Saddleback Resources and CLASS 301 (if you don't use those resources already). This is where you can find all the literature and materials related to finding out one's SHAPE (Spiritual Gifts, Heart, Abilities, Personality, and Experiences). I've taken spiritual gifts test in the past, and while a few of my spiritual gifts may be nearer the top, I found after going through CLASS 301 and the SHAPE process that some of those gifts were not my SHAPE.

Not only do you need to find a person that's SHAPE'd for leading your team, this also holds true for your team members. Someone may have the spiritual gift of teaching, but that doesn't mean they're SHAPE'd to teach junior high school kids. That's the way it was for me: I enjoy teaching, and it's one of my gifts, but at our previous church, I found that teaching fifth- or sixth-graders wasn't my Heart or my Personality. That's why it's important to sit down with each potential security team member and get a feel for their walk with Christ, their passions, their interest, their personality, and their interpersonal skills. They need to be SHAPE'd to serve on your security team.

Leadership titles or roles are easy to hand out but difficult to take back if you later find the person you've appointed isn't really suited for leadership. When you approach people you think would be suited to serve on this team, let them know you're putting a team together and see if they'd be willing to help—even if the person you're talking with is your first person. Once your team is put together, a natural leader will rise to the top.

Another thing to consider: Just because a person has a law enforcement background doesn't mean he or she is a fit for this ministry. I tell our new team members that security on a church campus is completely different from what it is on the streets. In fact, we had one team member who was a retired police officer, member of our church, and a great guy. But after some coaching, many talks, and much prayer, I explained to him that this ministry really wasn't his SHAPE and we got him connected to serve in another ministry.

Here's the downside to law enforcement: If 99 percent of what you deal with are negative situations—rapists, murderers, pedophiles, drug dealers, and so on—it's tough to not become cynical and jaded, and there's no place on a church security team for a team member with a cynical or jaded heart.

If you have prospective team members who are currently in law enforcement, have them check with their department(s) before they start volunteering. In our local area, many agencies don't allow officers to volunteer in a security capacity because the city attorney has determined that there is a liability exposure for the city.

Once you've come up with a group of people who are willing to serve on the team, meet as a group and lay out your vision and goals for this ministry. It's much easier to set the expectations in the beginning than go back and do damage control later on. In this first meeting, talk about how this is a ministry. And as we spoke of earlier, let them know that as part of their role as security team members, they need to be comfortable with praying with someone. Tell them that as a ministry, it's very likely this will happen.

A couple of other things I want to mention about security teams. A few years ago our team consisted of 11 people. We had five independent contractors—all of whom were retired or former law enforcement—that provided security during our weekend services and during the graveyard shift (11 p.m.-7 a.m.). We also had six volunteer team members who served in our security camera room during our weekend services.

During that season, we only allowed those with law enforcement experience to serve—either paid or volunteer—on our campus patrol team. As our weekend attendance grew, we realized we'd have to come up with more volunteers to adequately cover the campus. We tried recruiting some volunteers from among our members that were current or former law enforcement; however, we kept coming up against the same challenge with each one we spoke with. They wanted to serve their church, but because of their ever-changing schedules, they really couldn't commit to doing this.

At that point, we decided to open our security team to those without a law enforcement background. I could give you story after story of how well that is working, but one of the best examples is the volunteer leader of our security campus team—a guy named Mark. He has no law enforcement experience, but I can't imagine having any other person shepherding our volunteer security team. He does an amazing job.

Don't put yourself inside a small box. If we had maintained our previous mindset, we'd likely have a team of 15 or 20 team members. But with a lot of prayer and openness to whatever idea God would give us, our security team of 11 has become a team of 167 over the course of seven years. I'm constantly amazed at how God provides our every ministry need if we just ask him to show us how to solve the current challenge we're facing.

As a congregation, we have a number of people who serve in law enforcement. I hated the idea of having so much talent inside our worship center and not being able to use that talent, but as a former law enforcement officer, I totally understand that it's a very demanding career.

But we knew that if we were to ever have a mass shooter, any off-duty cops on our campus would respond—and we knew that the worship center would be a scene of chaos. So we came up with a plan that flowed from a conversation with a current law enforcement officer. I asked if he would be interested in serving as a volunteer on our security team and received a familiar answer: He was too busy. So I talked with him about the idea of a Law Enforcement Ministry, a serving opportunity for those currently in law enforcement. Once they arrived at a specific service, they'd check in with the lead security person and let them know where they would be sitting. Their role would solely be if we had a mass shooter.

This accomplished three things. First, it helped us identify some of our law enforcement members in each service. Second, it would definitely be a help to have more trained law enforcement personnel inside our worship center if—heaven forbid—we were to ever experience a mass shooter. And third, our pastor is always talking about getting all of our members serving in a ministry. So in this case, even a member with a heavy, chaotic schedule, could say, "Yes, I serve in a ministry; I volunteer on the Law Enforcement Ministry Team."

I'd also encourage you to think outside the box regarding your security team members' gender. Many people still think of this as a male role, and at some point I was likely of this mindset. But God has shown me over the past couple of years that women serving on our security team can be great assets.

Our security team is not intended to be nor will it ever be a police force. That's not our role, and that's not our goal. That being said, we do incorporate learnings, trainings, and some structure from our law enforcement backgrounds. One of those structural models is our leadership team. We have two leaders whose roles would mirror that of a sergeant. Our next level of leadership would be similar to the role of a captain.

This person on our security team at Saddleback is my right-hand leader, Gina, who has a background as a deputy with the Los Angeles County Sheriff's Department. Our security ministry team would not be what it is today without Gina's influence. God truly SHAPE'd her for this role. I've seen her use verbal judo to calm down and diffuse a verbally hostile person. And I've also seen her handle a situation tactically to the point that if someone came onto our campus with the intent of doing harm, I have no doubts that she would be able to handle whatever came her way.

Here is one more thought as you're starting your security ministry. Get in touch with your church insurance company and set up a time to meet with your insurance agent. Be very proactive with them, let them know your plans, and show them the policies, procedures, and guidelines you've come up with—and seek their input. It's vital that your church and insurance company are on the same page. We have spent a great deal of prayer, thought, time, and counsel creating our policies, procedures, use of force guidelines, and other guidelines. If you'd like any of these documents, I'd be more than happy to share them with you, just send me an email (kevinr@saddleback.com) and I'll send them your way. The only stipulation: If you come up with an incredible idea, please share it with us—we're always looking to learn and to improve!

4

Equipping a Team

This will be a constantly evolving thing, but before you start out it's a good idea to have some basics in mind. As we talked about earlier, you can start your team out without any financial resources.

However, down the road, as soon as you have some funding, there are some tools that you should have as soon as possible—and many tools you can add as your ministry grows.

To give you an example: A couple of years ago, we launched five new regional campuses for Saddleback to add to our existing three campuses. Each of these new campuses started out with a very small budget. When we talked about funding for security, we set aside resources for three two-way radios per campus. From a security standpoint, we were starting from scratch, so we'd have to wait until each campus grew before we could afford other tools. However, radios are foundational.

If you are on a limited budget, they don't even have to be high-end radios. I once bought a set on eBay® for a church to help them get started. I paid less than $50 for the pair. They were entry-level but brand-name radios and would do a fine job for what the church needed. If you can start out with just two, then issue one to your lead usher and one to whoever is in charge of your children's ministry. If you have a problem with a child or an issue with a non-custodial parent, at least the children's worker can get in touch with someone right away. And if you have a security team then start out with three radios: one to your security team leader, one to your lead usher, and one to your children's ministry leader.

At Saddleback we issue radios to our security team, ushers, healthcare team, children's team, traffic team, and our facilities team. Communication is vital for not only safety but for many other uses as well.

Please understand this next part is not intended as an endorsement of any particular brand—again, it's just what works for us. Use this information to then figure out what best suits the needs for your church. And don't let Saddleback's size affect any decisions you might make; it's all proportional.

That being said, we currently use more than 350 two-way radios at Saddleback. On any given weekend I'd estimate that 75 percent of those radios are used by volunteers.

Over the course of six service times and multiple venues during the two days, we have several people using the same radio. John, a volunteer on our Traffic Team, may use it while serving at our 4:30 p.m. Saturday service. And then Jack will use the same radio when he serves on the Traffic Team at the 6:30 p.m. Saturday service, and so on—you get the idea.

So those radios get a great deal of use—and sometimes abuse. When we first got into it, we had to either purchase a large quantity of entry- to mid-level radios that were fairly inexpensive. Or we could save, spend a bit more, buy them gradually, and buy more of a mid-range/higher-end radio. The latter is what we decided to do, and it's been a good choice. Because of how much abuse the radios take, if we had bought a lot of entry-level radios, they'd be in and out of the shop for repairs. That would not only cause us downtime, but at some point we'd also potentially end up investing more on repairs than the original cost of the radio.

We chose to go with Hytera PD702s. They cost a bit more per unit, but considering the amount of use and abuse, it's been worth it. They are built like bricks—not in weight, but in solidness. In any given year, we may have one or possibly two in the shop for repair. Given the number of radios we have and use each day, this is an extremely low ratio. There are many good name-brand radios out there; Hytera is just one of them and the one we chose to use. If you're just starting out and have limited resources to invest, get some good entry-level radios; they'll do the job just fine to start out. But as you grow, give some prayerful consideration to spending a little more on the front end with the desire of saving more in the big picture. As always, we want to be good stewards of every tool and every resource we have on our team.

In addition to the radios, I'd strongly encourage you to invest in headsets. This is a feature that can be added to almost any two-way radio. One of the most common and the kind we use is the headset used by the U.S. Secret Service. It consists of a small, internal ear piece, clear sound tube and wire that goes inside one's shirt or jacket, and a separate wire for a mic that can be run inside a shirt or jacket with the mic clipped and sticking out of the front opening of the wearer's shirt.

This type of mic is helpful because it minimizes interruptions—it would be disruptive to the worship service if a transmission suddenly came across the radio requesting a maintenance request due to a leaking toilet or sink. Or if someone on your security team received a transmission from Children's Ministry asking for help to locate a missing child, this would likely instill panic among any parents within earshot. Headsets remove those problems.

We equip our team members with other useful tools, too. Remember that we didn't start out with all of these things. It's been a journey, and I'm sure there are tools we aren't currently using that someday we will. But this will give you an idea of what we use and why we use them.

Firearms are not our most important tool; however, in talking with churches around the country, it seems to be one of the first questions asked, so I'll hit that one first. Before I go any further let me be clear on something: I'm not anti-firearms. I'm a huge Second Amendment proponent, I've been collecting and shooting firearms since I was 11 years old, and I believe that any adult with a clean background and training should have the ability to get a CCW (Carry Concealed Weapons permit.) Please don't misinterpret the following paragraphs as an anti-firearms declaration.

We decided that our policy regarding firearms and our security team would be this: The only team members that are allowed to carry a firearm while serving would be those with a law enforcement background.

It is my daily prayer and my hope that we never experience a mass shooter or any person using a firearm at Saddleback Church. However, if we do, any security team members that draw a firearm need to have the law enforcement tactical training and experience so they can react in the best and safest way possible.

I've heard the argument that "Joe" has been around firearms his entire life; he shoots all the time, is extremely safe, and is a very good shot. That's all good and well. However, if someone walks into our worship center during a service, pulls out a firearm, and starts shooting, "Joe" doesn't have the experience to respond properly and do what's necessary to stop the assailant.

We have a few team members that currently have CCWs or want to get one. We've let them know that's great for them personally, but while serving on our team they won't be able to carry their firearm.

The likelihood of a mass shooter in a church is very low. It does happen, but not too often. I just wanted to be sure you understood our policy on firearms on our team and why we came to the decision we made.

For your church I'd suggest you give this some prayer and a great deal of discussion, and then also check with your church insurance carrier. We were proactive and shared our policy with our insurance company, and they were in total agreement.

Before you finalize your policy on firearms and your security team, also check your state and local laws. In California we have the BSIS, Bureau of Safety and Investigative Services, a state organization that regulates security guards and other agencies. In California, paid members of our church security team have to be licensed by the state with a Guard Card. For our team members that carry firearms, they must get an Exposed Weapons Permit from the state.

Even though we carry our weapons concealed, we must get that permit. In California, per the BSIS representatives, these permits are not required for our volunteers because we are a

501(c)3 nonprofit. So make sure and check with your state's laws regarding this.

A few years ago we started talking about tasers and stun guns. The catalyst behind this conversation was an incident during a service one weekend. We had a male in his late 20s verbally disrupt one of our services. We later found out he was mentally ill, paranoid schizophrenic, and off his medication by choice.

In the service, this individual was verbally angry and combative, shouted profanities, and attempted to kick people sitting in their seats as the security team was in the process of removing him from the service. Our team removed him from the service, took him to an area outside the building, tried to calm him down, and waited for local law enforcement to respond. But he became more physically combative with our security team members. It was at that point the decision was made to place handcuffs on him to protect others and to also protect him from harming himself. It took a great deal of maneuvering to get him under control.

While debriefing later that day, we realized that situation could have gotten a lot worse and people could have been injured if the physical combativeness had happened inside the worship center or if he had been in a crowd of people on the patio before or after a service. It was this situation that led us to a non-lethal tool.

We had two options and chose a stun gun over a taser. This was our reasoning: If we found ourselves in a situation where this tool was needed, it would most likely be inside a service or in a crowd—based on the fact that we're a church. Our concern was most tasers from a distance look like a firearm. We didn't want to have to pull out that tool and here someone scream from 50 seats away "He's got a gun!" and then have a mass hysteria. Also, tasers use a small barbed dart connected to the taser by a small wire. I didn't want the risk of a 60-year-old woman sitting near the problem person getting tasered.

With a stun gun, if we had a physically combative person that we needed to remove from the service, this person can be escorted out by two security team members. If the person became a physical threat to others or to the security team members, one team member could fairly discretely place the stun gun against the thigh or side of the person, depress the switch, the person goes fairly limp, and they continue removing that person from the service area. This would protect the worshippers and the security team members from physical harm, as well as protect the person from getting hurt. Again, as with firearms, check your state and local laws regarding stun guns.

All of the tools our team members carry are carried discretely. And that leads me to a question I've been asked: "Does your team wear a uniform?" In the truest sense of a uniform, no. We issue medium-blue, camp-style shirts—the bottom portion of the shirt is cut straight across instead of having it longer in the front and back like a standard dress shirt. Above the pocket on the front we have embroidered "Saddleback Church Security" in grey thread.

The text is about 1-inch tall. We want to be recognized, but not "in your face" as security. Our style of shirt means we can leave them untucked so as to cover up the tools we carry. Again, it goes back to that mindset of not appearing as a heavy-handed security presence.

At a recent security conference where I was speaking, I wanted to express how you can come across in a very subtle way, from a security standpoint, while still being fully equipped to handle whatever might occur. To convey my point, I proceeded to remove item after item and set them on a table on the stage. First came the two-way radio—that was kind of a given because I was wearing a surveillance earpiece. Next came the handcuffs, then a container of pepper spray, pair of latex gloves, stun gun, and extra magazines.

I did stop prior to removing my Glock (for safety reasons) but let them figure that was the one item left.

My point was this: Other than the radio earpiece, no one would have any idea the tools we carry, and that's the way we want it.

We've talked about the individual tools our team members carry. Our vehicles are also tools. This is mainly due to the fact our campus covers a somewhat large area. But I've seen vehicles used in large, medium, and small churches. At our Saddleback main campus in Lake Forest, we have 11 parking lots plus buildings spread out around our campus. We started out with a golf cart for our security team, and then we acquired a Ford® Bronco. Yes, it was a late '80s white Bronco, and we took some good-natured ribbing because it looked like the one O.J. Simpson had ridden in, but all our vehicles are donated so we're grateful for whatever we get. Since that time we've been blessed to have three other SUVs donated (our Bronco motor finally gave out.)

We're running over 3,000 events on our campus a month, seven days a week, both night and day. We're located in a nice city in a relatively low-crime county, but it's a shock to some (those that live with their head in the sand) that crime happens in good neighborhoods, too.

One of our reasons for having the security SUVs is that we regularly have women's groups meet on a weeknight on our campus. If their meeting lasts until after dark, then we have women walking at night through parking lots to get to their vehicles. Anytime these events are scheduled, we'll have one of the security team members that's on—whether they're paid or a volunteer—spend time driving through the parking lots, just being a presence and a visual deterrent to criminals.

So if we weigh the cost—donated SUV, "Security" on the doors in vinyl lettering, a used light bar bought on eBay®, and the 15 or 20 minutes of a security team member just driving around the parking lots—it's pennies compared to the sense of safety we provide and the feedback we get from the women attending the events.

That's the reason we have church security teams, isn't it? To provide the safest environment we possibly can, and to minimize disruptions and disturbances we can so those that come to worship and learn can focus on that experience. That they don't have to worry about other things, and if there is a disruption, we resolve it with minimal disruption so people can go on doing what they came to do in the first place.

Another idea we wanted to implement was a bike team. Since I took over this role as head of security at Saddleback, we've only had two vehicles broken into during weekend services or meetings. But if we can make that number zero, I'd be happier. So we bought a mountain bike (eBay® was cheaper than Target® or Wal-Mart®), had it lettered ("Saddleback Security"), attached a headlight and a bag (with first aid kid and campus map showing the buildings), bought a helmet and a polo shirt, and one of our guys rides through the parking lots during services. The idea was that an extra security presence would help deter potential crime in our parking lots. But this person also provides directions to new people on our campus. I knew that tactically this would be a useful tool and also good from a public relations standpoint. What I didn't realize was how high the positive PR would be.

After about five weeks of having our bike in service, one of our bike team members told me he'd had families stop him on five different occasions and ask if they could take a photo of the family—and they wanted him and the bike in the photo. Go figure! I believed the PR would be positive, but didn't figure at this level. We started marketing this to our security volunteers and picked up three who said they wanted to switch from the campus security team to the security bike team. So we added another bike.

And right from the start, we've had people approach our security bike team members saying how they liked the bike idea and how they appreciated the fact that Saddleback was thinking "green" and conserving fuel by using bicycles on our security team.

Three years into it, we now have eight bikes and about a dozen volunteer team members that ride. We've had team members tell us that they love serving on the security team, and now they get a cardiovascular workout while serving.

A side note on our security bike team: We bought helmets (white, which are cooler and stand out for safety's sake), gloves, and white polo shirts. We wanted our guys recognized as security but didn't want it to be a "billboard" either. On the front of the polo shirts, about where a pocket would be, we had "Saddleback Church" embroidered (same as on our campus patrol team shirts.) We had someone suggest we have "Security" silkscreened in large print across the back. But we decided not to go this route.

If you go this route, find a shirt made from material that keeps moisture away. This will help your team members in the summertime. And consider tactical polo shirts that have penholders sown into the side of the sleeve. This made it easier for our guys to carry a pen for writing. These seem like small details, but they made a difference.

I met with leaders from a church in Colorado; their weekend attendance was about 500, and we helped them start a security ministry. Their church sits on about 10 acres, and has three buildings and a couple of parking lots. The church isn't in a bad neighborhood, but they've had some problems in the past with people breaking into cars and local kids riding their BMX bikes through their planters, jumping them off planters, and tearing up their landscaping. We got them set up with a plan to start a security ministry.

A few months went by and I got a call from the pastor telling me how their security ministry was working. One piece of it was really nice: They approached a local bike shop, told the owner what they were wanting to do (they were hoping to get a discount on the purchase of a bike), and he ended up donating all they needed to get started: a bike, helmet, gloves, lights, and a bag.

A couple of weeks later, their volunteer was telling this pastor a couple of stories. One was about a family that was driving around the parking lot on a Sunday morning, apparently searching for an open parking space. Because it was 10 minutes into the service, you could see the stress on their faces. The security team member stopped them, had them follow him in their car while he rode his bike, and led them to an open parking space he'd seen moments before. Now that's service!

The second story was even better. One Sunday morning he was riding his security bike around the property while the service was going on. He encountered four boys riding their BMX bikes through the planters. He stopped them, asked their names, and then mentioned to one of them, "That's a nice bike you've got." A couple of the boys (who were in their early teens) said the same to him about his mountain (security) bike.

They talked about disc brakes, dual suspensions, and local places to ride. Once he'd built rapport with them, he said they were more than welcome to be at the church, but when they rode their bikes through the planters and through large puddles in the grass, it tore them up. The boys apologized. So what did this security guy not do? Well, he wasn't heavy-handed, and he didn't ride up yelling, "Hey you kids, get out of here! You're tearing up our property!" No, he approached them and, as my pastor says, built a bridge and let Christ walk across.

Fast-forward to the best part of the story. That security volunteer happens to love mountain biking and rides with a group of guys from their church each Saturday. God placed it on his heart to start a ministry where he could use that experience to minister to teens. They now have a mountain biking ministry, and they invite anyone that would like to ride with them. Those four boys that were riding their bikes through the church tearing up the landscape now go on the Saturday rides with the church group.

They also get together every so often and teach the younger guys bike maintenance, such as adjusting derailers, brakes, and other bike tune-up things. Oh, and I saved the very best part for last: Two of those boys now regularly attend that church's youth ministry.

All of this happened because a church decided to think outside the box, set up a security team that had a foundation as a ministry (as wise as serpents and as gentle as doves at the same time), didn't come across heavy handed, and used it as a bridge-building opportunity.

5

Training a Team

Training is as crucial as a strong foundation, and it serves multiple aspects. First, as we say, we prepare for the worst and pray for the best. We train and hope that we'll never need to use the training, but we still train. We do multiple types of trainings throughout the year. We do annual, biannual, quarterly, monthly, and impromptu trainings each year. We came up with a list of all the training topics we thought would be applicable to what we need.

We created an overview of each training topic, and then in November of each year we create our training calendar for the upcoming year. Here is a list of the trainings we do and the description of each one.

Mass Shooter Training
This training encompasses the basic skills utilized in engaging and stopping a deadly threat on the Saddleback Church Campus. Each church-approved team member who carries a concealed firearm is required to attend this training no less than three times per year.

The team members will learn how to engage and stop the threat(s) as quickly and safely as possible. We use realistic physical scenarios to give the team members a better grasp of what can actually happen during an active shooter event.

The goal of this training is to equip the team members with the skills necessary to end the threat in the safest and most expeditious manner possible, which, in turn, will minimize the casualty rate during the incident.

Detain and Control Handcuffing Techniques

This training teaches the team members the proper way to detain and control a subject who is uncooperative and/or combative. The team members learn how to approach, detain, control, and subsequently handcuff a subject while keeping themselves as safe as possible.

Control holds are taught to gain control of a subject who is a potential danger to the team member or guests. The control holds consist of wrist locks and arm locks that limit a combative subject's movements. This limited mobility of a subject gives the team member the ability to now handcuff a combative subject if necessary.

Handcuffing techniques are designed to assist the team members in safely and effectively handcuffing a subject. The techniques taught incorporate balance and control holds, and keep both the team members and subject's safety in mind.

Bike Training

This training is designed by the bike leaders and incorporates riding through obstacle courses, patrolling the campus using the safest routes, and how to check up and maintain your bike and equipment. The training also teaches the bike team members how to be more aware of their surroundings while riding so they can be as safe as possible.

Each bike team member must pass the bike training in order to ride for the Security Team.

Building/Room Searches

The team member is taught the safest way to enter and search a room or building while on the church campus. The training goes over both occupied and unoccupied buildings. We complete room and building entries/searches using one-, two-, and three-person teams. This gives the team members a variety of techniques to use while working at church.

Child Custody and Civil Disputes

The team members are taught the laws surrounding child custody disputes between separated parents. They are taught the proper way to handle the issues of separated parents trying to pick their children up from Saddleback Kids, when they were not the parent that dropped them off.

If the parent does not have the check-in/check-out ticket from Saddleback Kids, then they do not have the authority to pick up the child/children. If there is no court order stating parental rights, then OCSD (Orange County Sheriff's Department) may have to be called in to assist.

A civil dispute on our property not involving our church employees needs to be referred to the OCSD, unless the parties involved can reach a mutual agreement.

Our team members will not get in the middle of child custody disputes or civil disputes. We will merely stand by to keep the peace in these situations.

Consensual Contacts

The team members are taught the proper way to approach persons at church during a consensual contact. They are taught the reasons we make contacts (i.e. suspicious individuals, possible mentally ill persons, couples arguing, and so on).

Our goal is to teach the team members the safest way to make contact with the individuals without drawing too much attention from the other guests on our campus.

Counselor Training—Dealing With EGR Guests

We have one of our certified church counselors conduct training with all of our team members regarding how to contact, converse, and minister to our guests requiring extra grace.

These EGR guests can be withdrawn, upset, and sometimes violent. This training will assist our team members in dealing with the EGR guests in the safest way possible.

Flashlight Safety Skills—Usage and Tactics

This training will teach our team members the proper use of flashlights while working on the church campus. We have a lot of dark areas in our buildings, and having a working flashlight is an important tool to have at all times.

The flashlight training will teach proper maintenance and usage of lights while conducting searches and low-light contacts of individuals on our campus that require our attention (such as unauthorized personnel in our buildings or on campus when campus is closed).

Interviewing Techniques

This training teaches the proper way for a team member to conduct an interview of individuals regarding incidents on campus.

They will be taught to ask the appropriate questions that pertain only to the incident being dealt with. They will know to get the individual's name, address, birthdate, and other information in case the incident turns into a crime report.

The interview techniques being taught will assist the team members in getting the important information needed without detaining the individuals for a long period of time.

Live Fire Training Drills

This training is only for our church-approved team members who carry an approved Concealed Carried Weapon while working on our church campus. The training will be at an approved shooting range and will teach the proper movements while holding their weapon at the ready position. It also teaches how to shoot while moving, shooting from behind barricades, and team movement drills while shooting.

This training will be given by the Director of Security's approved range masters, who will oversee all firearms training. The weapons will be checked before and after training to ensure that they are the approved duty weapons for church.

The range masters will confirm the weapons are clean, oiled, and in good working condition prior to the beginning of training.

The goal of this training is that each team member can shoot on the move, know how to utilize their cover and concealment and what the differences between the two are, and have the confidence to engage an active shooter should the worst-case scenario at our church occur.

Observational Skills Training—Head on a Swivel

This training will teach the team members to always be aware of their surroundings while working on church grounds. The team members will sometimes transport money across campus and need to be aware of subjects approaching from all different angles. These subjects may be trying to rob or assault the team members for their bags of money.

They will also be taught the proper way to address guests that may try to stop them and ask questions during their transports. We need to be professional and let the guest know that we will be right back to assist them but have to take care of something first.

They will also be taught how and what to look for in a suspicious subject and how to go about contacting that subject in a safe manner. As the team members walk the campus, they need to be aware of risk management issues such as raised pavement tripping hazards and fire lanes being blocked inside and outside of our buildings on our church campus.

Officer Safety Tactics

This training will teach ways to stay safe while on foot, bicycle, and vehicle patrols. It will show our team members the proper ways to defend themselves in a fight, should that arise. It will also teach the proper ways to calm individuals before a physical altercation arises, which is the goal of our security team.

The training will show the team members various weapons used by the "bad guys" so they can better prepare and defend themselves during these types of contacts.

The goal of this training is to give team members the proper mental attitude and skill set to handle these volatile situations with the safest outcome possible.

Radio Etiquette

This training encompasses the proper usage and terminology for our radios. The team member will learn how to use the radio as a communication tool instead of a conversation tool. They will learn to only say what is needed and not use up radio time that might block someone else who might be trying to call for help on their radio.

They will learn the proper radio codes to cut down on talk time and also to hide certain radio traffic from other ministries possibly listening in.

The team members will learn the proper way to attach their radios to their belts and the proper usage of their headsets so we do not broadcast our traffic out to those who do not need to know what we are doing.

Range Qualification

The team members who are authorized to carry concealed weapons while working at our church **MUST** qualify four times each year at either their police agency (if they are still active duty) or at On Target Indoor Range, where Saddleback Church has set up an account.

The church pays both for days of range time, ammo, targets, and for the time that the team member is there. The team members must shoot from 21 feet from the target and get all rounds on the target to pass qualification. The target will then be brought to the training supervisor for approval. The receipt from their range qualification also needs to be turned in to the training supervisor.

Report Writing

The team members will be taught the proper way to write their incident and crime reports so they put all the pertinent information needed. They will be shown how to check spelling and grammar after their report is completed so it is clear and concise. The team members need to know that the reports they write could possibly be used in court and need to reflect the professionalism of our Security Team.

Vehicle Approaches

This training teaches the proper way to approach parked occupied vehicles during foot, bicycle, and vehicle patrols. It will teach the safest way to pull up to a vehicle while in the Security SUVs, carts, and bicycles. It will show the proper way for one or two team members while on foot to approach the vehicle from different angles to ensure the safest routes of contacting persons inside the vehicle.

The team members will be shown how to look for suspicious movements inside the vehicle they're approaching and also how to retreat from the vehicle while maintaining a position of advantage should the consensual contact turn violent.

Verbal Judo

Each paid team member has been given the *Verbal Judo* book by Dr. George J. Thompson and is responsible for reading and using the techniques taught in the book.

Verbal Judo gives the team members a different way of contacting difficult individuals by using non-threatening techniques to diffuse a situation before it gets worse. The book gives great tips on how to talk to individuals and how to arrive at a solution to their issues without going hands-on, if at all possible.

Weapon Cleaning and Maintenance

The team members who are authorized to carry firearms while on church property will be taught how to keep their weapons cleaned, oiled, and functional.

They will be taught the proper weapon disassembly and reassembly in order to keep their firearm in proper working condition. This will also make them more comfortable with their firearm so they can handle any problems that can arise during a shooting (such as stove pipes, failure to feed, and failure to eject casing).

Weapon Retention

The team members will learn how to keep their weapons from being taken by an aggressor. The team members will have an adequate holster, and they will be proficient in its workings and will be confident that they can retain their weapon while running, jumping, and climbing.

If the worst-case scenario happens and someone gets their hand on a team member's weapon, they will be taught the proper way to disengage the suspect's hand from that weapon and clear the suspect away from them. They will be taught how to take the suspect into custody utilizing approved takedown techniques.

Shoot Don't Shoot

The team members who are authorized to carry a firearm will go through the PRISim simulator training system a minimum of one time per calendar year. This training is conducted by Self-Defense Firearms Training located in Huntington Beach, California.

Those are the training topics we have to date. In addition, we do the trainings required by CA BSIS in order for our team members to maintain their Guard Cards and Exposed Weapons Permits.

We have been blessed with team members who have a great deal of law enforcement experience. However, we also contract with a retired Los Angeles Police Department officer who trains church security teams for a living. We bring him in once a quarter and conduct trainings on handcuffing techniques, powers of arrest, and crowd control.

Once you have your team up and running, I strongly encourage you to consider hiring an outside source for some training. In our highly litigious society, it's all good and well for your church's legal counsel to be able to state your church security team does a great deal of training.

When the plaintiff's counsel says, "Sure, but it's all in-house training," your counsel can rebut that with the fact that in addition to all the extensive training conducted in-house by your team, they also contract with an independent law enforcement training specialist.

6

It's All About the Kids

In my mind, our children are the most important reason for having church security. Can we ensure that nothing will ever happen with our kids? No, but we can do our due diligence to provide the safest environment possible. And I believe we have a responsibility to do that. While parents worship with other adults, they entrust us with their children, so we need to provide an environment where they feel 100 percent comfortable and can worship without the mental distraction or worry about their child's safety.

I put in lots of hours and learn, train, and strive to make Saddleback Church as safe and disruption-free as possible for one reason. While I may report to my boss, our director of campus operations, I answer to God. Someday God will say, "I gave you this ministry to lead and to shepherd. What did you do with it?" This is what motivates me and keeps me striving to do the best I can to serve God. I don't want there to be a day when God says, "If you had only done this or only put this system into place, this wouldn't have happened to that child."

As church staff and leaders, we're entrusted to shepherd those God puts in our path. Not only are we to help them grow spiritually, but we're also entrusted to keep them as safe as we possibly can, to provide that safe environment where they can grow closer to God. There are so many things we can do, so many procedures we can put in place. Please don't let costs keep you from doing this.

First, these things can be done with minimal cost. Second, let's take the "God holding us accountable" factor out of it for a moment. If you fail to put systems and procedures in place and something happens to one of the kids in your care, do you really want to be the one to explain things to the upset parent(s)? And third, if something bad happens in your children's ministry and it likely could have been avoided if you'd put systems in place, will parents feel comfortable bringing their kids to your program? Of course not.

If my family and I are attending a church and I find out a child was touched in an inappropriate manner by someone who had been convicted in another state as a pedophile but this church didn't do a background check before letting this person volunteer on their children's team, do you think I'm ever bringing my child back to that church? Again, of course not.

So let's talk about some foundational procedures that should always be put into place, starting off with background checks. We do a background check on everyone who serves on our children's team or youth team (paid or volunteer). We use Live Scan, but there are many other good companies out there that provide this type of service, so get connected with one of them. Most registered sex offenders are fully aware of their restrictions and limitations and comply with them. However, I sure don't want to be the church that doesn't check and finds out later that a registered sex offender realized background checks weren't being done and decided to volunteer on the children's team.

As a matter of fact, we do a background check on anyone that remotely serves around kids. We do checks on our security team and anyone on our audio/visual team that takes care of the videos and sound during our children's services. We simply don't want to allow or permit any situation where children might potentially be at risk.

We use a "Check In/Check Out" system for our Saddleback Kids Ministry. Please don't think this is an overwhelming system and it takes a great deal of resources. Regardless of the size of your church or the limits on your financial resources, this can be done. And more importantly, from a biblical stewardship standpoint, we don't have a choice—we're commanded to protect these little ones, so we have to make this a priority.

When a parent brings their child to one of our children's classrooms to check them in, we already have returning children in our database, and if it's their first time, we'll enter them in the system. The check-in process generates a sticker with the child's name on it, which is placed on the child's shirt. A duplicate sticker is given to the parent. Once the service is over and the parent returns to pick up their child, they present their sticker and their child is released to them.

In addition, our kids are trained to take off their sticker before they leave the classroom and give it to the teacher. This eliminates the chance of them still having it on while standing outside the women's restroom when mom is inside, and a stranger coming up and being able to use the child's name in a conversation.

I've personally encountered our process at Saddleback Church in a rather humorous way. One weekend my wife and I checked our youngest daughter into her classroom. They scanned our card, and the computer generated and printed out two stickers, one for our daughter and one for us.

Susan and I attended the adult service, and after it was over, Susan stopped to talk to a friend for a moment so I volunteered to pick up our daughter. When I got to her classroom, I stood in line with the rest of the parents waiting for my turn. But when I reached the front of the line and the volunteer worker asked for my sticker, I realized Susan still had it. The volunteer said, "I'm sorry, I can't release her to you without the sticker. Can you wait until your wife gets here?"

I should have known to ask Susan for the sticker. It was my fault. And how ironic: I'm the head of security here and I can't pick up my kid—but this volunteer was totally right. Then one of our Saddleback Kids staff team members came up and told the volunteer, "That's Kevin, he's our head of security here" right about the time Susan arrived and gave the volunteer our sticker. The volunteer scanned the sticker and said, "I apologize, I didn't know who you were," and I replied, "No apologies necessary—you were doing your job, you did the right thing. Thank you for being so careful."

A few years ago, I was helping a church in the Southeast set up its security ministry. They'd flown me out to spend a few days with their leadership team. During one of our initial meetings, we started to talk about security and their children's program. This was a church of about of about 500 adults and about 100 kids. I asked them if they had any check-in, check-out system in place for their kids program. Their children's director said they really didn't have anything in place—but they were small enough they knew all their families and they knew all their kids. They didn't think they'd really have any problems.

I said, "Okay, let me paint a hypothetical scene for you. John and Mary have been members of your church for many years. Their two children, Jane and Jack, have been attending your children's program for at least six years. One Sunday morning Mary drops off Jane off in her sixth-grade class and then drops Jack off in his fourth-grade class. Mary is a little quieter than usual, but no one notices it. She attends the adult service, and when it's over, she picks up Jane and then goes to pick up Jack. When she arrives at Jack's classroom, she notices he's not there, but figures someone's taken him to the restroom.

"She is greeted by the class volunteer, and when she asks about Jack the volunteer says, 'Your husband came by a few minutes ago and picked him up. He said something about taking him for ice cream and meeting you guys later.' Mary becomes panic-stricken and says, 'The kids and I left last week; we went to my parents' house. John's been drinking again and has been physically abusive. He said he was heading to his parents' house in Texas.' Now Mary's afraid that John has taken their son out of state. Sure, it would have been helpful if Mary had told you guys about this when she dropped her kids off. But the week had been emotionally devastating for her and it didn't occur to her. It's one more reason to have some form of system in place regarding the kids we're entrusted to shepherd."

In addition to background checks, there are other simple things you can put in place to ensure the safety of children. Always insist that there are at least two adults at a time in each classroom with the kids. This also serves to protect the adults from any accusations. If you don't have enough leaders on a particular weekend to have two adults in each classroom, then combine a couple of grades for that weekend rather than putting only one adult in a particular classroom. At Saddleback we have "junior" leaders—typically, teens that want to help serve with the kids. That's fine, it does satisfy the two "leaders" in a classroom, but we don't allow them to be alone with the kids even if the leader needs to leave for just a minute.

I would highly encourage you to come up with a policy regarding the reporting of suspected abuse of a child in your care. If any of your children's ministry team notices bruising on a child or through general conversation is concerned there might be abuse going on in the home, this needs to be reported to local law enforcement. Many times it will turn out that it wasn't abuse; perhaps the child was punished (in a fair way) for bad behavior and is looking for a way to get back at the parents. However, I'd always rather err on the side of caution and have an embarrassed parent or child than not say anything and have abuse continue. NO child should ever have to experience that.

What about bathroom breaks? We do restroom breaks in groups of three or more. It is always a leader that's over the age of 18. This person will take at least two kids to the restroom, never just one child. And we also limit the number of kids to a maximum of four per adult.

Code Alex is a concept we implemented in the event of a lost child. Prior to each service, our security team will designate which security team members would respond to and post at the south end, north end, east side, and west side of our children's building if a child is reported missing. Then another security team member will be the point person and connect with the children's staff team member to ascertain the missing child's name, age, description, and areas last seen—virtually throwing a "ring" around the children's building. The other security team members will fan out to other areas of our campus searching for the child.

7

Handling Disruptions

We've been running into this issue more and more. As with everything else we do, it always needs to be handled in a Christ-like way, being as wise as serpents and as gentle as doves. Our disruptions have included angry persons who don't like Christians, legalistic Christians who think churches don't do enough, people struggling with mental health issues, and people that just want attention and want to speak to our congregation. In each situation, no matter how EGR they are, they're treated respectfully. That doesn't mean we just sit there and watch them disrupt the service, but we seek to approach, handle, and interact with them in a Christ-like way.

When someone is creating a disruption, we have two security team members respond, and if the person is seated in the middle of a row, we have a couple of ushers accompany them. The ushers' role is to get the attendees who are seated between the person creating the disturbance and the end of the row out of the way so the security team members can move in and interact with the person.

For us, nine times out of ten, the person causing the disruption expects that they will be asked to leave and they comply when the security team members request to speak with them outside. We do this in as discrete and orderly of a manner as possible. I've reviewed security camera footage after the fact, to see if we could have handled things better, and each time I'm so impressed at the professional and Christ-like ways our security team members handle situations.

One situation from a Sunday morning service comes to mind. One of our team members, Mic—she's currently a police officer with the LAPD and also serves as one of our part-time paid staff members—was seated in our "Position Two," one of our front-row seats in our main auditorium. Early on in the service, she was alerted via radio by one of our security camera team members that a woman seated in the middle of the front row just seemed to catch their attention. This person seemed nervous, fidgety, and hyper-focused on Pastor Rick.

Near the end of the service, everyone stood up for the final song, just prior to the offering. Mic kept this woman's mannerisms and body language in her peripheral vision. The hope was that this person just had a hard time sitting still. However, while the song was still going on, this woman put one foot out and it was obvious she was heading toward the stage—and Pastor Rick. Mic immediately moved forward, placed an arm around the woman's waist, and talked with her as she gently guided her back to her seat. The woman picked up her purse and Mic picked up a bag she had with her, and the two of them walked out one of the side doors to the patio outside.

We got comments and questions from volunteers and attendees along the lines of, "That was so nice of that security team member to help that woman" and "Was that woman okay? She seemed upset." What they saw was a security team member helping, serving someone.

Mic told me afterward that the woman said that God has spoken to her in a dream and she had information she needed to share with Pastor Rick. Mic explained that Pastor Rick was busy with the sermon, but if she'd come outside, Mic would be more than happy to find a pastor she could talk to. We have pastors and ministers available before and after every service, to talk and pray with people. Anytime they see a member of the security team escort someone out of the worship center, they're great about meeting them and helping out. Mic was able to get this woman connected to a pastor who sat down with her, spent some time talking with her, and prayed with her.

What did I see when I reviewed the videotape? Because everyone was singing, no one could hear the conversation between Mic and this woman. All they saw was a security team member helping and comforting a woman. As Mic and I reviewed the footage together, we watched as Mic—in a very Christ-like, loving manner—put her arm around the woman's waist, comforted her, and guided her away from the stage and back toward her seat.

I turned to Mic and said, "Nice job, you were really caring about her—and discretely checking her for weapons, weren't you?" Mic replied, "Yes, sir." I noticed a similar thing as the woman picked up her purse and Mic helped picked up her paper grocery bag. Mic had taken that opportunity to make a quick, unobtrusive visual search of the contents of the bag, making sure it didn't contain any weapons. As wise as serpents and as gentle as doves—textbook.

Things don't always go that calmly or quietly. About a year ago, we had a guy attend one of the Sunday morning services who intentionally seated himself in the middle of the middle section. During the beginning of the service when everyone stood to sing, he stood and sang along with the rest of the attendees during all three songs. But when the music was over and everyone began to sit down, he remained standing. In a voice just short of yelling, he began declaring that the church didn't do enough to talk about the evils of homosexuality and abortion.

The moment this started, the security members nearest him headed his direction, with a couple of ushers right behind them. He continued his rant about how churches must preach and shout from the stage how evil homosexuals and those performing and having abortions were. The ushers quickly got the people sitting in the same row on that end out of their seats and into the aisle. Our security team members went in and, upon reaching him, took him by the arms—in a control hold, in case he might attempt to physically lash out at anyone seated in the rows in front or behind him—and escorted him outside.

Our security team members who serve in the security camera room had already contacted the Orange County Sheriff's Department, and they had a deputy on the way. Upon arrival, the deputy spoke with this person, getting all his information, and then advised him that he was trespassing on private property and if he came back, he would be arrested.

Again, wise as serpents and as gentle as doves. The reason it went so well was because our security team members are constantly training again and again, their role-playing of these types of scenarios, their high degree of professionalism, and their Christ-like hearts to serve and to protect in this ministry.

8

Soft Target/Hard Target

This is an area where you can make a difference many times with no financial investment at all. Let me first explain the meaning of a "Soft Target" and a "Hard Target." The "Bad Guys" want a Soft Target—a location that's not well-secured, doesn't have good lighting at night, doesn't have people who are aware of their surroundings, has people that haven't given any thought to their safety and/or the security of their property, or allows young children allowed to wander around the property (such as trips to the bathroom) alone without any adult supervision. To people with bad intent, this is a Soft Target and one they seek out.

The opposite, a Hard Target, is a location where a potential criminal runs a high risk of being noticed, runs into all kinds of stumbling blocks (including locked doors and well-lighted external areas at night), and encounters consistent supervision of young children, just to name a very few things. This creates an environment where a person with bad intent will give up and move on to seek a Soft Target. Unfortunately, due to convenience, denial, forgetfulness, and sometimes laziness, some churches have unwittingly placed themselves in the Soft Target category.

In my mind, it's not really a "responsibility" issue from a financial or bad PR standpoint. It's a biblical issue, a topic of stewardship. Whether it's protecting the "sheep" that God entrusted us to care for, or it's being wise about the "tools" and resources God has loaned us, it's a stewardship issue. As Scripture says, those that can be trusted with much will be given much.

Some churches tend to focus their defense only on the big items—the people, computers, audio/visual equipment—and pay no attention to the small things, such as chairs, ice chests, patio furniture, and so on. I remember working with a church in Pennsylvania a few years back. They expressed their frustration with the thefts they'd had over the past year—not big-ticket items, but many smaller-cost items.

They didn't know that when I arrived in town the night before, I did a site assessment of their campus, and I arrived a bit early for our meeting that morning and walked around their campus. I took some pictures and made some notes of things I observed. I'd downloaded the photos and added them to the PowerPoint presentation I'd created for them.

The following are just a few of the things I noticed or found during my site visit the night I arrived. Sitting on a walkway outside a classroom was a new-looking, 35-gallon Igloo ice chest. Sitting outside a storage shed was a nice-looking Honda push-type gas lawn mower. Behind their storage building were stacks of cases of bottled water and canned carbonated drinks. Outside the front door of their office was a metal drop box (with a flip-up lid, not a locked lid.) When I looked inside, I found two tithing envelopes in the box, each with a name handwritten on it. The envelopes were sealed, so I had no idea if they contained checks or cash. On a patio were groupings of patio furniture, chairs, tables, and umbrellas.

And the best one: I found one of their classrooms unlocked; it appeared to be a third- or fourth-grade classroom. In that room I saw the standard classroom supplies you'd expect to find. But I also found a laptop, a small computer projector, and an iPod. By the way, I did lock that classroom door on my way out!

When I showed the church leaders my findings, they were shocked. Each finding had an explanation. The ice chest was used at a recent event, thus the drinks left out, too. The lawnmower belonged in the lockable shed, but was likely forgotten and left outside. The classroom was a teacher who was in a hurry to leave.

I told them that those things made their church a Soft Target. When I drove onto the campus, I saw the ice chest from the parking lot—it got my attention. Those things can be $90 items. So once I saw the ice chest left out, if I'd been a criminal, it would have caused me to look around for other "left out" things—and I found an open "shopping trip" of things I could steal and either use personally or either pawn or sell.

I told them they didn't have to become paranoid, just wise. Putting things away in a secure location—that's a slam dunk. But if they've had thefts in the past, and they also wanted to have patio furniture for their members and guests to sit on, then they could get some cabling and locks, run the cable through them, and lock them at night. Could the cable or lock be cut? Sure, but now they've made that patio furniture a Hard Target. Criminals would have to bring a pair of bolt cutters or find a church that didn't lock theirs together. Same with the drop box—if they want to provide this convenient way for people to drop off tithes and offerings after hours, then install a mail slot and have the envelopes fall inside the locked office. The leaders got my point.

In regards to security being a stewardship issue, this is what I tell my team. During one of our team meetings I talked about how we are called to be good stewards of each item, each tool, and each resource God had loaned us. I had them close their eyes and I was going to "paint a picture" for them to mentally envision. I had them picture a single mom in her 30s standing next to her three kids, ages 11, 9, and 6. She's divorced, receives no child support from her ex-husband, and works two jobs to support her family. Then I asked my team to visualize her at church. She's sitting in one of our seats and writing out a check, her tithe, which she faithfully does every week, and she puts it into the offering basket. Her tithe helps pay for all the tools we use, all the resources we purchase, and, for those that are on staff, it pays for our salaries. We owe it to her and all those like her to be good stewards.

9

Partnering With Local Resources

This is such an easy idea. I can't believe it's not utilized more often, but I know why it isn't: Most church leaders don't think of it! Look for ways to partner with local police and other law enforcement!

The law enforcement agency that takes care of us is the Orange County Sheriff's Department (OCSD.) Those guys do an amazing job! We've "partnered" with them in multiple ways. First and foremost, we thank them. Every year or so, we'll coordinate with their time schedule so we can take lunch to them. In our situation, we have a food ministry that caters all of our campus events, so we make the lunch in-house and deliver it. However, you could just as easily contact your local police department, find out how many officers and support staff are working on a particular day, and take them lunch from a sandwich shop or another inexpensive restaurant. It's a meaningful way to say thanks for what they do for your community.

We've also benefited from an invaluable service they provide, at no cost: They sent someone out to do a threat assessment of our property. There were many "problem" areas we were aware of, but the deputies who surveyed our campus came up with many other observations that were extremely helpful. This gave us an active law enforcement assessment of our campus, showing us any weak areas. It also gave the deputies that conducted the assessment a firsthand look at our property and buildings. The chief later arranged for all of his deputies that patrolled our city to meet with us and do a walk-through of our property and buildings. That way, if they ever had to respond to a call from us, they were already familiar with our campus.

We also let them know that they could use our property on an evening and do building search training, and they were more than eager to accept our offer. This has been beneficial on two fronts: One, it is a bridge-building, relationship-building opportunity. It helps them by offering a real-life location to train. Two, if we ever had a problem in our main office or another building and they had to respond, they're extremely aware of every aspect of that building.

Also ask your local law enforcement agency about meeting with your staff and doing some training on personal safety while at work and in the world. Make it a lunchtime meeting for your staff and the officer. I'm sure they'd be more than willing to do that. We've done that for our staff.

With all the things listed above, you've built a relationship with your local law enforcement agency. You can create opportunities to appreciate and love on them. If you ever need to call them for help, they'll willingly respond and help you out—that's what they do. But in your case, it would be different because this isn't just an address or a business in their city—these are their friends at a specific church.

We've done the same with our local fire agency, the Orange County Fire Authority. As Pastor Rick Warren says, there's only one thing that really matters in life: relationships. Having a relationship with Christ and having relationships with others.

10

Security Cameras

Let me start off by saying that a security camera system can be a great tool. Over the years, we have built our system up to well over 250 cameras. However, I caution churches considering security cameras that they serve a specific, valuable purpose, but the presence of security cameras should never replace other security measures. They can be a great supplement, but should not be your sole focus.

To the honest person that's on the fence about doing something dishonest, they can be a visual deterrent. However, we've all seen videotaped footage of robberies at local convenience stores where the bad guy was fully aware he was being videotaped and committed a crime anyway.

Still, there are many positive reasons for having a security camera system. For example, we have video cameras in each of our nursery classrooms. This protects our staff and volunteers from a child/parent claiming something happened that didn't. This also provides a check-and-balance system for our volunteers, which protects the young children we've been trusted to care for.

Another benefit is the ability to view video footage after the fact. Many times we'd had something turn up missing or something happen, and we've been able to view video footage from a particular camera, letting us determine specifically what happened and who was involved.

Our security cameras have been incredibly useful during our weekend services and large events, too. We have been blessed with an incredible group of people who serve on this team. Each weekend they serve at our two Saturday evening services, our Sunday morning services, or our Sunday evening service, and they typically serve twice a month.

We have three camera stations in our security camera room. Two of them have 65-inch monitors, and one has a 48-inch monitor. Throughout the service, this team monitors different areas of our campus, both outside and inside buildings. They have been instrumental in finding lost children, helping keep us apprised of vehicular traffic flow on our roads, and have noticed individuals in the worship center that ended up having interactions with our security team members. Whether the person approached the stage or caused a disruption, our security camera team members are often the ones that first spot a POI (Person of Interest).

Please don't think that your church's size or budget means you can't have an effective security camera system. It took us many, many years to get to the point where we are currently today. But with the advances in technology, a church can purchase a simple, entry-level security camera system for a fairly reasonable price.

If I was just getting started and had limited resources, I'd start off with a DVR (digital video recorder) and four fixed-position cameras. PTZ (pan, tilt, zoom) cameras are more expensive, and having a PTZ is really only advantageous if you have a person sitting at the camera workstation that can move and reposition the PTZ. So I'd start with fixed cameras.

As to placement, I'd place one in the room that was used as a nursery. Then I'd place one in the room where the tithes and offerings are processed. Third, I'd place one in the front lobby of the main office looking toward the front door or lobby. And I'd place the fourth one in the main worship center, facing the direction of the main entryway doors. As you continued to grow you could add more cameras, another DVR and eventually move from a DVR to an NVR (network video recorder.)

I hope that you were able to glean some tips and ideas that can help you in forming or fine tuning your security ministry. If you have any questions about any information in this book please feel free to contact me via email at kevinr@saddleback.com. Most of the churches I've worked with have found that forming a security ministry team is actually less difficult than they'd thought and the idea that it requires a large financial investment was not the case. As pastors, I believe that along with helping our members continue to grow closer to God in their daily walk, serving him, and serving others, another part of our responsibility is to keep them as safe as we possibly can along with providing as disturbance-free of a worship environment as we can. Sadly, in this day and age, this means we will likely have the opportunity arise where we find ourselves in need of having a security team at church. It's kind of like the fire insurance policy we have on our homes. We hope and pray we never need it; however, if we have a fire, we want to know it's there. Same with a church security ministry: We prepare for the worst and pray for the best and hope we never need it.

Acknowledgements

God has put so many people and opportunities in my life, and each one of them has helped to shape me to the person I am today. I could fill pages with all my acknowledgments, but I'll keep it short—and if you've impacted me but I don't mention you here, please know that you are in my heart and thoughts.

First and foremost, I thank God. Thank you, Father, for creating me, loving me and saving me—I love you so much. Thank you, Rick Warren—my pastor, my mentor, my friend, and my boss. You listen to God each time he speaks to you, and he's using you to change eternity for more people than we can even imagine. It is such a privilege to serve under your Christ-like leadership. Thank you to my incredible security team—you are the ones that make it happen, and I love serving alongside you. My fellow Saddleback staff members, you truly are my family; I love each and every one of you. Pastor Steve and Pastor Abel, your friendship is a gift from God. My friends Glenn and Karen, thanks for providing the environment to write this book: the arena, the stalls, the horses—it recharges my batteries and was the perfect "canvas" for me to write on.

And my family, you have been so graceful, you've supported me each and every day, and you've seen this as I have: not a job, but a calling. My incredible wife, Susan—you've worked for decades in a field that's not your favorite, but you do it so I can serve at our church. You have one of the biggest, unselfish, Christ-like hearts I know of. My daughters, Tawny, Megan, and Sophie—thanks for sacrifices you've made as pastor's kids, thanks for the grace when I work Christmas Eves, Easters, Civil Forums, conferences, and other times. I am so proud of each one of you, and one of my greatest joys is being your dad.

My sons-in-law, Joe and Jon—thanks for being such good husbands to my daughters; to a dad, this means a great deal. Thank you to my grandkids, Joey, Jayme, Brenna, and Declan—you make me smile, you are my legacy.